M000045829

Discipline Yourself

Develop Habits and Systems to Boost Mental Toughness, Conquer Self-Sabotaging Behavior and Finish What You Start

(The Key to Getting Things Done)

Pollux Andrews
polluxandrews@gmail.com

TABLE OF CONTENTS

Chapter 1: Introduction

Have you ever had a dream that seemed so difficult you thought it would be impossible to achieve? If so, did you pursue your dream or let it pass away with time? Many fall into the latter category, but there are others with similar dreams who summon all their willpower, passion, and energy into achieving those dreams.

What separates those who dare to dream and risk it all for success versus the ones who give up and let their dreams fall into obscure memories that make for regrets later in life? The succinct answer came from none other than Theodore Roosevelt, when he said:

"The one quality which sets one man apart from another—the key which lifts one to every aspiration while others are caught up in the mire of mediocrity—is not talent, formal education, nor intellectual brightness—it is self-discipline."

You don't have to live a life full of regret. Don't let your past consume your future. With self-discipline, you will be able to face your fears, conquer your distractions, and stay focused on your end goal. To achieve self-discipline, one must first open their mind and be willing to assess their physical and emotional selves. This can be a difficult but rewarding process, and not everyone who attempts this makes it out on the other side without fully armed with self-discipline skills. It is a process, and processes take time to see results. If you're familiar with the term "practice makes perfect", then learning self-discipline will be all about drilling those habits into your brain, until they become second-nature.

This book aims to show you how to build your self-discipline and apply it in every facet of your life. At first, it will seem daunting, but soon you'll realize that through installing few habit and persistence, you too can master your mind, impose self-control, and achieve your goals faster than ever before. The key objective of this book is to help readers find their self-discipline and provide answers for those that are struggling to achieve their dreams.

Firstly, you will learn in the book why do you succumb to your temptations and **what drains your willpower**. The book will teach you further **how to design an environment** that promotes self-discipline by making little tweaks in your surroundings.

You must have heard the quote by Jim Rohn, *"Motivation is what gets you started. Habit is what keeps you going."* Therefore, you will find one full section on the **developing habits** that will help you in strengthening your willpower. Since this book is meant to be a practical resource, you will also learn **how to build foolproof systems** that safeguard your willpower. You will also find **practical strategies to incorporate self-discipline** in different areas of your life in the last section of this book.

Let's start with the fundamentals of self-discipline.

Chapter 2: Fundamentals of Self-Discipline

Almost every success story brims with self-discipline, as you have to be determined to accomplish your goals. That tenacity, that drive you have, can only be met with self-discipline otherwise you won't be able to complete your goals no matter how hard you try.

Knowing the fundamentals of self-discipline now will make it that much easier for you learn how to use your willpower, positive self-talk, and more. There are many ways to explain how self-discipline works, but let's illustrate things with the following story, which might be thought of as cliché, but that's likely because it's a common one that people can relate to.

There were two brothers, Mike and Brian. Mike, the older one, was a dreamer. He was an artist and dreamed of having his own business one day. He wanted to make custom signage for the local businesses in his community. Mike was a very good artist and he knew a lot of people in town. Some were friends who were business owners; others were owners of places he frequented.

His first few clients were impressed with his work and success seemed imminent to him. Mike worked out of his apartment and enjoyed the freedom of owning his own business. But soon, like so many other independent entrepreneurs, Mike started feeling pressed for time and strapped for cash, so he had to dedicate all his time and energy into every aspect of his new business himself. This eventually took its toll on him. Over time, Mike began to feel overwhelmed. Finally, without much income from his new venture, Mike called it a day and shut down his business after only a few months of "living the dream".

However, in stark contrast to his brother, Brian, was a doer. Like Mike, Brian wanted to own a business, too. A few years prior to Mike's dabbling in entrepreneurship, Brian had recognized a missing niche in town—a specialty food market. He was still in school at the time, learning how to track trends and pull market data when he first hatched his own idea.

He spent the next couple years compiling research, building a concept around his brand, filing the necessary local, state, and federal documents for his business. After graduation, Brian shadowed a few local business owners who owned a food truck, and one very successful coffee shop. Once he had his business plan complete and he knew he had done all he could, Brian felt confident he was ready to start his business.

All his perseverance and nose-to-the-grindstone attitude would pay off. He knew he had a winning solution to this missing market. Within its first year of business, Brian's specialty grocery was thriving, and his community received it well. He gave the people what they wanted, and he was able to do it because he had the self-discipline to make it happen. His long years of preparation couldn't have been possible had it not developed self-discipline in his behavior. He could have easily digressed and reacted on his impulses or would have given in to temptations at the young age, but he chose to exercise self-control, that helped him to work single-mindedly on his worthy business pursuits.

Mike's failure wasn't because he lacked the ambition or talent to run his own business, it was because he lacked the self-discipline to follow through with his business. Moreover, Mike was a little too free-wheeling to have any structure, something that a business needs, and ultimately, he fell victim of being overwhelmed and giving up, almost before he got started. Now, Brian's story is one where his self-discipline is what carried his success. He started developing his idea early on and spent a few years doing all the legwork that he knew he'd have to if this was going to happen. When Brian saw the opportunity to learn about something new related to his future entrepreneurial endeavor, he learned it. He shadowed. He asked questions. Short of self-sabotage, there was nothing stopping Brian's success. How many times have you done this?

What is it that made Mike different from his brother Brian? It could've been that Mike simply didn't have the same drive as his brother. Or maybe he couldn't follow through on his dreams. Or maybe Mike wasn't honest with himself about his dreams. Whatever the factor(s), Brian reaped success and all the benefits of his hard work, whereas Mike fell to the wayside and watched his so-called dream crumble. Mike was not wrong in his decision-making per se but had he incorporated the level of self-discipline Brian had pushing him, things may have turned out differently for him.

This story was meant to be both inspirational and a cautionary tale, as it shows the pitfalls of following your dreams as well as the potential payoff. If you keep your eye on the prize, you'll realize that your goals are all that matter, and you'll accept nothing short of seeing your goals realized. You're willing to put everything on the line and risk it all for success. While it's great that Brian was successful thanks to his self-discipline, we can't discredit Mike, the part of the story we don't know is whether or not Mike tried to start another business after that. Remember, it's not over just because you fail. The ability to fail and try again is an exercise, albeit a painful one, in self-discipline. What about you? Are you like Mike or Brian?

To help you introspect better about your behavior and actions so far in life, one more example will help you understand the right perspective. Perhaps an even more relevant story might be the one about Katie, who started developing her self-discipline routine in college, where she was studying to become a biochemical engineer. This was already a difficult profession to get into, and her field was dominated by men, but Katie was determined to achieve her goal.

While in school, she practiced her daily morning routine of waking up early, going for her morning run around campus, showering, getting dressed, and eating. Sometimes she would add a quick study session if she had a test that day. Katie's middle name was "multitasker" and while she had many different things to do, her routine provided her the much-needed order she'd have to possess to be successful. When it came to her studies, Katie maintained a particularly strict routine, as her classes always came first: *No parties. No dates. Period.* Some may think she was harsh on herself, but her diligence and willpower overcame any indulgences she might've had during her study-time.

While Katie's story is not unique, many people struggle with their lack of willpower and the ability to exert control over their impulses. Katie grew up in a household where chores were a part of daily life, and she learned self-discipline at an early age. She always accomplished what she set her mind to, and college was no different. Katie was determined not to let anything derail her as she tried to successfully navigate the obstacles of college life.

We all know a Katie, Mike or Brian in our lives. Which of them are you most similar to? If you find yourself identifying with Mike, you may need to evaluate what your core values and goals are before you leap into something that gets you in over your head. As Stephen Covey said once:

"You have to decide what your highest priorities are and have the courage — pleasantly, smilingly, non-apologetically — to say "no" to other things. And the way to do that is by having a bigger "yes" burning inside."

If you identify with Brian or Katie, you understand how difficult having self-discipline can be. But right now, we're not going to worry about the Brians and Katies out there, we want to help the Mikes of the world, who have it in them to succeed, but just need that extra boost of self-discipline to put them over the top.

It takes a healthy dose of self-discipline to succeed in any area of life, whether it's your physical or mental health, work or career goals, or your everyday relationships. Let's first understand what we mean by self-discipline.

What is Self-Discipline?

In what is probably one of the best definitions of self-discipline, the self-growth website IQ Matrix[1] defines it in below words:

"Self-Discipline is about the ability to control your desires and impulses for long enough to stay focused on what needs to get done to successfully achieve your goal.

---

[1] https://blog.iqmatrix.com/self-discipline

It is about taking small consistent daily actions that help you form critical habits that support your objectives."

Having self-discipline isn't just about consistently doing something, instead it's about systematically regulating, correcting, and adapting your behavior to the changing conditions and circumstances of your life.

Self-discipline, is, therefore, effectively about proactively training yourself to follow a specific set of rules and standards that help you shape and align your thoughts and behaviors to the task at hand.

Learning self-discipline is to learn about gaining control of your willpower. You might ask what the difference is between willpower and self-discipline as they seem similar. Here is the difference. While *willpower* is your ability to keep your mind under control, *self-discipline* or self-control is the action of consistently doing the required action or avoiding something despite distracting unworthy temptations.

As per American Psychologist Association[2], some psychologists define willpower as the ability to delay gratification, resisting short-term temptations in order to meet the long-term goals.

Roy Baumeister, a researcher on willpower defines willpower and explains its significance as below:

"Willpower is what separates us from the animals. It's the capacity to restrain our impulses, resist temptation — do what's right and good for us in the long run, not what we want to do right now. It's central, in fact, to civilization"

Your willpower enables you to make the right decisions that will move you towards your goals. While willpower is something everyone has, not everyone's willpower is ignited by the same things. For instance, if you were interested in baseball and not physics, you're going to put all your willpower into learning how to become the best ballplayer you can be, whereas you may not have the willpower to succeed in physics. This is arguable, of course, but

[2] http://www.apa.org/helpcenter/willpower.aspx

when people are most passionate about something, they have a stronger willpower to accomplish their related goals.

A lack of willpower is a lack of control, the very control you need to take charge of your life situation. Willpower and so-called "mental toughness" are nothing more than interconnected parts of a whole, both of which work together through conditioning. For you to complete your journey of mastering self-discipline, you will need to learn the skills of conditioning your willpower, to make it work for you rather than against you.

How is Self-Discipline proven to be necessary for long-term success?

There is a now-famous psychological test from the 1960s called the Marshmallow Test conducted by Walter Mischel and his graduate students at Stanford University's Bing Nursery School, where children were presented with a choice between the instant gratification of eating one marshmallow immediately, or waiting twenty minutes and receiving two marshmallows. This was meant to be a predictor of a person's willpower throughout their life, and Mischel even followed up with the original children as adults to see if the test's hypothesis was correct.

It turned out if a child took the single marshmallow, they ended up having a more difficult and unstable life. The impulsivity that caused them to take the instant gratification of the single marshmallow stayed with them, and in fact grew with them, into adulthood. Likewise, the children who chose to wait for the larger reward tended to fare better than their impulsive counterparts later in life. Many of them had stable careers and family lives, and many believed that they had a strong willpower in general. Researchers discovered that parents of *high delayers* even reported that they were more competent than *instant gratifiers*—without ever knowing whether their child had gobbled the first marshmallow.

How many times have you been confronted with a situation where you couldn't tell yourself "no"? For many of us, it is a daily struggle, but practicing willpower not only has a positive effect on your decision-making, but it also provides better consequences in the long-term.

Goal-setting for Building Self-Discipline

While it's important to never lose sight of your ultimate goal(s), it's also important to simplify your goals, strip your goals down to the bare minimum. This will enable you more easily focus on the daily rituals that you need to build up step-by-step to attain the level of self-discipline you want to have. It's wonderful to have big, singular goals that you can stay fixated on throughout the storm of daily life, but it's also good to have micro-goals, that is goals that are smaller and more easily attainable but work together towards completing a larger, overarching goal. From the self-discipline perspective small goals are a good starting point, if you are beginning your journey towards self-discipline, because you don't feel overwhelmed.

Remember, you're setting the coordinates for your journey, and if you don't have the proper coordinates, you'll get lost at sea. That's the idea behind goal-setting whether these are long-term goals or short-term goals. In fact, the short-term goals are nothing but the connecting points to the long-term objectives of your life.

One more thing, goal-setting is easy if you're honest with yourself about what it is that you want. How else are you supposed to know what you truly want out of life if you can't be honest about what you want? Self-discipline is a necessary exercise in both stages i.e. setting your goals and then achieving your goals, so you can focus on what's important and what isn't. Think of this as your chance to lay out all your hopes and dreams on the table. That can be scary for many people, so the best way to approach this is to think big and whittle down to most realistic and feasible goals you can actually work towards with some sort of endgame in mind.

You know the saying: *"It is always best to start at the beginning; you have to learn to walk before you run; baby steps."*

Self-Discipline Makes Your Happier

Not only self-discipline helps you to work towards your goals in a more focused way, it makes you happier too. Wilhelm Hoffman and his team of researchers at the University of Chicago conducted a study[3] in 2013 and discovered people with high self-control are happier than those without. The study explained that because the self-disciplined subjects were more capable of dealing with goal conflicts. These people spent less time debating whether to indulge in behaviors detrimental to their health and were able to make positive decisions more easily. The self-disciplined did not allow their choices to be dictated by impulses or feelings. They simply don't waste time fighting inner battles over whether to eat a second piece of cake. Instead, they made informed, rational decisions daily without feeling overly stressed or upset.

To summarize, self-discipline is something that paves the way towards achieving your goals, it makes you feel in control of your destiny instead of becoming a slave to your circumstances. It puts you in the driver's seat, you are no more victim of your circumstances, because your willpower

3

https://www.theatlantic.com/health/archive/2013/07/study-people-with-a-lot-of-self-control-are-happier/277349/

becomes the key to take untiring actions towards your dreams. In a way self-discipline is the key to ultimate freedom. That's why Aristotle rightly stated once: *"Through Discipline comes freedom"*.

Jocko Willink, former Navy SEAL commander also mentioned; *"Discipline equals freedom."*

Finally, you wouldn't find any better summary of how willpower can change your life other than what Kelly McGonigal, a researcher and author from her book *The Willpower Instinct* states:

> We may all have been born with the capacity for willpower, but some of us use it more than others. People who have better control of their attention, emotions, and actions are better off almost any way you look at it. They are happier and healthier. Their relationships are more satisfying and last longer. They make more money and go further in their careers. They are better able to manage stress, deal with conflict, and overcome adversity. They even

live longer. When pit against other virtues, willpower comes out on top. Self-control is a better predictor of academic success than intelligence (take that, SATs), a stronger determinant of effective leadership than charisma, and more important for marital bliss than empathy (yes, the secret to lasting marriage may be learning how to keep your mouth shut). If we want to improve our lives, willpower is not a bad place to start.

Throughout this book, you'll learn a bevy of new self-discipline tips and techniques that will show you how to find your willpower, how to exert it, and when to apply these newfound self-discipline tools as you begin to see patterns emerge with repetition, as well as learn more ways that self-discipline can help you succeed.

For now, let's move on to understand the psychology of temptation and the factors that drain your willpower before you learn the effective ways to acquire and master self-discipline skills.

Chapter 3: Temptation All Around Us

When it comes to self-discipline, many of first think of self-control. Whether it's money, substance abuse, sex, or anything else that someone could have trouble with. The things that tempt us in life are generally temporary. If you have strong self-control, it may be easier for you to turn down any temptations that come your way.

According to the American Psychological Association, humans have "a limited reservoir of willpower", which could mean that if we are bombarded with too much temptation, we eventually end up slipping. Temptations will come in many forms, and ultimately, it'll be up to you to make a decision if and when the time comes. This could be a business venture or a romantic relationship. Or buying a new car or house when you know you can't afford it.

Willpower also can be compared to a gas tank and you can't have an infinite supply of willpower. It's bound to run out, so you need to choose it wisely.

Psychologist Roy Baumeister from Case Western Reserve University states that willpower is like a muscle and gets fatigued by using it. Like the body gets tired by physical work, willpower exhausts by mental work and he conducted an experiment in 1996 to test this phenomenon, which is known as *willpower depletion.*

In the experiment, few participants were divided into two different groups and they were sent to a closed room. Now one group was offered freshly baked cookies and other sweets, and the other group was instructed to eat bitter radishes. Also adding to the whammies of the radish eaters, they were forced to sit along with a cookie eater group in the same room and you can imagine how strong the temptation would have been for them. The first part of the experiment finished when each group had eaten their respective portion.

Now the second and important part of the experiment started. Both groups were now taken to another area and each of them was given a totally unrelated task to test their level of persistence. They were now asked to solve a complex geometric puzzle. The radish eater group was not able to focus on the solving the puzzle even less than half times than the cookies eater group. In other words, the cookie eater group were persistent and used their willpower for more than 200% as compared to the other group.

The results of the study clearly indicate that the group who had to resist the temptation for longer used a lot of willpower in resisting, and therefore they were not able to engage themselves better in another complex task, as their willpower tanked. It proved that willpower is a limited resource, and it needs to be safeguarded for better pursuits.

However, most people unknowingly remain trapped in a mediocre way of living, because they exhaust their entire willpower in following unworthy pursuits, simply by getting lured to every temptation. Such lack of self-control in the face of unworthy impulses often has terrible after-effects.

Here's a story of Terrence, who otherwise had his life together—a good job, a girlfriend, a nice apartment. Terrence had something else though, an impulse disorder that caused him to engage in undesirable behaviors such as kleptomania, sex with risky partners (cheating on his girlfriend), and alcohol abuse. Terrence's story isn't uncommon, think of someone like Terrence as lacking self-discipline. From the onlooker's perspective, Terrence may have it together, but he really is one impulsive mess. If he is going to get himself together to reflect what everyone perceives him to be, he's going to have to tap into his reservoir of willpower to break out of the impulsive lifestyle he's been leading.

For Terrence, there were many triggers for his impulsive behavior. Whether it was swiping a candy bar at the checkout or flirting with someone new. His inability to say "no" would eventually come at a cost, but in his case, there were three major consequences—his girlfriend caught him cheating and left him; he was arrested for petty theft, which after court costs left him $1,300 in the hole; and because of his legal trouble, lost his apartment. Terence's story may be extreme but it's meant to serve as a warning for those with similar impulsive behaviors.

Every life decision you make has not only an immediate effect but also a ripple effect. With temptations, a moment's decision could affect your life down the road (e.g.; drugs and/or alcohol, casual sex, etc.) and many times you can avoid setting yourself up for disaster simply by exerting a strong willpower. Having (and using) a strong willpower means you can control even your most tempting urges before making a decision that could have negative effects on your life.

Avoidance

We cannot let temptation rule over chances of success. When you're working towards your goal, one of the best ways to not succumb to temptation is to avoid it altogether. This may be considered extreme by some measures, but if you recall the old adage *out of sight, out of mind*, you know that you can't be tempted by something you can't see. Tim Ferriss also supports this principle when he says:

"I value self-discipline but creating systems that make it next to impossible to misbehave is more reliable than self-control."

Avoidance is useful on several levels. First, avoidance can be used to keep ourselves from engaging in behaviors or situations that keep ourselves or others safe. Avoidance can also be a tool to turn away from those tempting moments that you otherwise would engage in. Typically, avoidance can stop your most impulsive moments from occurring, however, not all temptations are created equal.

Most of our impulses are traced back to our physiological ancestors, and we have only recently started to understand how our impulses work on the neurological level. Emotionally, we understand that impulses can be controlled, as it is behavioral, and behaviors can be altered through a variety of proven exercises and repetition of those exercises. Avoidance is a powerful tool for not engaging with temptations, again for obvious reasons.

EXERCISE: Think of a temptation that you may have in your life. Now think about what would happen if you give in to the temptation. Next, brainstorm ways you could avoid the temptation. Finally, have a contingency plan in case your first line-of-defense fails.

For example, let's say you were dating someone and you recently broke up, but you shared friends and frequented the same places, and you don't want to run into them. A good plan-of-action for this situation would be to (a) avoid those shared places at times when you think they may be there; (b) check with your shared friends to see if they are around before you go hang out; or any other things you feel might be effective to avoid your initial impulse to do something you may regret.

Interpersonal relationships can be difficult for some people, particularly those with impulse control issues. To stay on the dating topic for a moment, many people struggle with infidelity. The person accused of cheating sometimes literally cannot control themselves, because their impulses are telling them (unchecked by their willpower) to go ahead and do it anyway. This scenario plays out with addicts of all types. In an addict's mind, whatever serves the impulse is what is needed, be it booze, tobacco, or drugs.

The Psychology of Temptation

On a psychological level, your emotional state changes when you are presented a temptation. Typically, as adults, our brains are developed enough that we can control those impulses. What is the difference between a person who fantasizes about doing something impulsive and someone who actually does the impulsive thing? The answer is a lack of impulse control. This may be if the person is mentally ill or has a chemical imbalance or brain damage. Children are good examples of having a lack of impulse control, with their need for immediate gratification, which subsides the impulse once it is sated.

Lisa was like any other girl in her early twenties. She went to school, had a part-time job, hung out with her friends, and liked to go shopping. Lisa was always an impulsive girl. She was caught stealing when she was twelve and never did it again.

She was able to refrain from that despite her impulse to steal, because she knew the consequences and didn't want to tempt fate. Instead, her impulses became satisfied through spending. Lisa wasn't the happiest person, but she loved shopping and she spent every penny she earned on things. She still was not happy and had not figured out that void yet, so she continued to shop. Then, one day she realized she was broke, she had things she didn't want or need, and was still unhappy. She compensated for her unhappiness with shopping. Whether it was clothing, makeup, or other items, she purchased them with abandon.

To stop herself from falling into further despair, Lisa tried telling herself *"you don't need it"* whenever she wanted to buy something impulsively. She began to do it so often that she grew annoyed with herself to the point she simply continued walking past her impulse-buys in the store. She had to focus her willpower even more at the checkout counter, as she was tempted by all the items purposefully stocked as (and aptly named) impulse-buys. By using her willpower though, she was able to overcome her impulsive behavior.

What does this tell us about Lisa and people like her? It reveals that despite her impulses, she was able to summon enough willpower to stop her. It also shows that with practice and patience, self-discipline is possible, even for those of us who don't believe they have the willpower to overcome their problems in life or achieve their goals.

Once you understand the neurocognitive mechanisms behind your decisions and behavior, it makes it easier to form a strategy to overcome it. Also, while it can be difficult, it's not impossible for people with extreme cases of impulsivity to overcome their temptations and be successful. The work will be difficult but rewarding.

When the children in the Marshmallow Test did the test, they were unaware that their willpower was being tested, and those who were able to exert their willpower then, continued to be able to do so throughout their lives. That being said, there seems to be a limit to the amount of willpower we have and are able to use, and there are many factors that can, and will, drain your willpower. Let's now understand various the factors that cause to drain your willpower.

Chapter 4: Factors That Drain Your Willpower

Earlier, we talked about your willpower being a reservoir that essentially can be drained if you're presented with enough temptation. These temptations could arise due to extraneous factors as well as there are few psychological inner factors that drain your willpower. Some extraneous factors that could drain your willpower are:

- **Drug and/or alcohol abuse** is a factor that affects many people, and many feel powerless to stop. Drug addiction and alcohol abuse are diseases, and the addict is not always the one to blame, but they are the only ones who can change their own behavior. Using willpower can help in curbing addiction, or better yet, in preventing would-be users from ever starting down this dark path.

- **Risky sexual behavior** that can cause major health issues for you and your partner(s), including HIV and a host of other sexually-transmitted diseases. Sex addiction is a very real thing that millions around the world suffer from. Any dangerous or high-risk sexual activity can wreak havoc on your health and wellbeing, and however tantalizing the offer, this urge must be resisted.

- **Potential gains in financial status (i.e.; business deals)** can drain your willpower as well. If you are willing to risk it all to come out on top, you may cause collateral damage in your wake. The potential gains of your business deals will cloud your decision-making. If you're impulsive, that can negatively influence your decisions, which could be detrimental depending on the context. Remember, in business, being able to use your willpower will help you see the long-term and avoid making any hasty, shortsighted mistakes.

- **Potential gains in social status (i.e.; relationships)** can also drain your willpower as relationships become intimate and you may drop everything for the impulses of love and lust. Think about teenagers when they first experience romantic crush; they are each hanging out with their own friends one day, and the next they are with their crush; soon, every day; eventually their relationship is revealed to friends; they are boyfriend and girlfriend, a "couple". This will test your willpower with the immediate gratification of being labeled with a new social status versus holding off to see how things progress naturally, that is without interrupting your daily life.

These factors are dangerous territory for many of us, but gaining the willpower needed to overcome these potential hazards that will absolutely drain us of our willpower is an essential step to completing your journey to master self-discipline.

EXERCISE: Make a list of any factors that could drain your willpower, leaving you vulnerable to temptation. Once you have your list, write down all the ways you can ensure that these factors will not affect your willpower.

For instance, if you struggle with drugs or alcohol, the most effective way to not fall into those temptations is avoidance, however, you may not always be able to avoid it or the people around you who may still engage in those behaviors. That's when alternative plans are needed to salvage your willpower. Think of some ways other than avoidance you can use if you find your willpower confronted and being tested. This book does not mean to infer that willpower alone is enough to conquer addiction. If you have an addiction and need help, seek help immediately with your local crisis hotline or other emergency service.

Psychological Factors Responsible For Draining Your Willpower

There have been studies and experiments that show that you drain your willpower due to some psychological factors within yourself. Below are some of those inner factors that lead to willpower loss:

Stress Eats Willpower

Researchers in Switzerland did an experiment where they asked people to choose a food to eat, after the individuals had experienced moderate stress. Results showed that the participants were more likely to pick a food that tasted good, and less likely to select a healthy food that wasn't as tasty, when they were under stress.

This study also showed the neural pathways in the brain that influence a person's desire for immediate gratification show increased activity following moderate stress, whereas the brain areas that help control willpower and that affect the desire to maintain a long-term goal, such as healthy eating, show reduced activity. The results shed light on why the brain finds it hard to resist temptation even in people with good-health intentions.

That's the reason you'd have experienced that in the state of stress, most of your choices are unhealthy, because your willpower batteries are discharged. You get tempted to smoke or alcohol or indulge in another kind of binge-eating, etc.

There was a research conducted by researcher Megan Oaten[4], on students to see the effects of

---

4

https://guilfordjournals.com/doi/abs/10.1521/jscp.24.2.2
54.62276

examination-related stress on their normal body and mind functioning.

The participants were required to answer some questions that were devised to ascertain the level of their stress and how that impacted their self-control behavior in different activities. The result of the study indicated that when these people had some stress related to an examination, it had taken a toll on their capacity to control emotions. There was a rise in caffeine consumption, smoking, alcohol, and the intake of healthy food was significantly reduced. Even these people couldn't perform well in their routine household activities and couldn't discipline themselves to take care of their well-being-they didn't do their regular exercise due to stress.

Lack of Sleep:

The deficiency in sleep during the night makes people less resistant to unhealthy foods, and even results in more pleasure from indulging in bad habits.

In one study the researchers scanned people's brains while the people looked at pictures of different types of food. The "reward center" of the brain in sleep-deprived participants lit up more when they looked at unhealthy foods than at healthy foods. Also, it lit up more than the reward center of well-rested people looking at unhealthy foods.

Such situation is very difficult, because on the one hand, stress wouldn't make you sleep better, and the direct adverse impact of lack of sleep will be self-control. Therefore, you need to take help of some techniques like meditation and exercise (explained later in the book) that will calm down your mind and increase blood circulation in your body to enable you to sleep better.

Decision Fatigue

As you know now that willpower is not an infinite reservoir available to us. Each decision costs willpower, be it a big one or a small one. The more decisions you make, the less willpower you'd be left with for your remaining decisions. Psychologists call this concept decision fatigue.

You decision-making muscles get tired and your willpower drains. Either you don't make any fresh decisions, or you tend to make faulty decisions. You would notice super achievers understanding this concept. That's why you'd see Mark Zuckerberg wearing same color t-shirt and jeans every day, as this helps him to save his willpower to make bigger decisions. In the context of safeguarding the willpower for making bigger decisions, Barack Obama[5] once responded to a reporter about how he made faster decisions; he said: "You'll see, I wear only gray or blue suits. I'm trying to pare down decisions. I don't want to make decisions about what I'm eating or wearing, because I have too many other decisions to make."

One other study conducted on judges in Israel proved the concept of decisions fatigue. The study showed that judges were making positive decisions early in the morning almost 65% of the time, and by lunchtime they started to avoid making decisions or passed negative orders. The study concluded that in the morning, the judges took favorable decisions and granted parole to criminals. But as the day passed by, their willpower would tank by making many such decisions; thus, causing

---

decision fatigue, which affected their ability to make more decision – hence either they avoided making decisions or made the wrong decisions.

You now know the factors that can drain your willpower, and therefore would want to take precaution to avoid such drainage. To help you out, the next chapters of the book will help you to design systems, develop habits etc. to safeguard and improve your willpower.

Chapter 5: Designing An Environment To Encourage Self-Discipline

Your environment comprises of multiple factors including family, colleagues, the home conditions, workplace situations, etc. These factors are not always designed to get the best out of you; instead if you are not intentional, you will easily get swayed away by the temptations thrown upon you by your environment.

Your environment can significantly influence who you are, that's why it's so important you surround yourself in an environment that encourages self-discipline. You need to design your environment in such a way that it is conducive to protecting your willpower. You will improve your effectiveness if you can take control over those environments, shaping them into the type of environment that is both conducive to your level of self-discipline and allows for the growth of your willpower.

Self-control is often easiest when abiding by the old saying, "out of sight, out of mind." Removing all temptations and distractions from your environment is a crucial first step when working to improve your self-discipline.

What does a self-discipline environment look like? Your environment should be calming and free of as many distractions as possible so that you can focus on whatever task is at hand. It is understandably going to be an arduous process as you make decisions on what you keep in your self-discipline environment and what to purge. If you're having trouble thinking about this yourself, here are some tips on how to design an environment to encourage self-discipline:

- **At Home** is where you should feel most comfortable. If any of your environments can be aligned to be more conducive to growing your self-discipline, your home is literally the place. Developing self-discipline at home will give you the necessary, practical skills to overcome any latent self-disciplinary issues that could develop elsewhere because of unresolved issues at home.

For example, let's say you're chronically late for work, and not just a minute or two late, but significantly late. Every. Single. Day. If you develop self-discipline around this problem, you would set your alarm each evening before bed, no excuses. But what if you're notorious for sleeping through your alarm? Arrange your environment so that maybe you'll need to get up, get out of bed, and cross the room to turn the alarm off, thus waking you up. Or maybe you have trouble falling asleep. Build your self-discipline so that you remove all screens an hour before bedtime and stick to it. Your willpower will keep your impulse to check that email before you doze off. Practice your self-discipline at home daily and settle into your habits, which will also make it easier to practice self-discipline at the workplace and elsewhere in your life.

- **At the Office** your workspace can be adapted to better encourage self-discipline, including making better use of your time, utilizing parts of your work day to answer emails, and of course, staying off social media and your mobile device unless it's work-related. The last one is a tough one for many people because we are enamored with our phones and much of that time is spent on social media. Not only is an unproductive waste of valuable work time, it feeds the impulse that defeats your willpower. While it's not always that easy to do, these work temptations must be avoided at all costs!

On a positive note, workplaces already tend to have some structure (because chaos is never a good quality for a company to have), which will make it easier for you to apply your self-discipline skills in the office or at the job site. If you're really having trouble getting rid of your addition of social media notifications, download the SelfControl app on your computer to block distraction websites - Facebook, YouTube, even email - for a set period of time. Patience is another self-discipline skill that can be fostered in the workplace as work can get hectic and you start to get frazzled from being overwhelmed. With patience, you'll learn to take things on one-at-a-time as they come. Otherwise, you won't be able to exert any more willpower since you'll be drained at that point. At work, self-discipline is developed by practicing patience and perseverance. (Don't worry, though. It might seem daunting at first, but you'll have this down in no time!)

- **Your School or College** is a great place to develop your self-discipline as it is generally your first time away from home; it's a transition into young adulthood. It's an exciting time for many, anxious for others. Developing your self-discipline skills can be difficult due to all the distractions of college life, being independent for the first time, and all the other trials of young adulthood. Due to being younger, there are still many impulses ingrained in the young adult's brain. With many of those impulses still there, it will take time to shed those impulses, which can be overcome with a little self-discipline.

You have to want to make the needed changes to not fall prey to your impulsivity, and to do that you need to create an environment at school that is conducive to your studies and promotes self-discipline in your daily life. Some of the ways you can create a more encouraging school environment would be including preset study times for each of your classes that you will strictly adhere to (no last-minute Friday-night parties), attending all your scheduled class times (even if you don't want to), and maintaining a proactive interest in your academics (visit with a counselor, apply for scholarships and internships, etc.)

- **On the Weekends** is a time when many of us "cut loose" and we tend to let our self-discipline fall to the wayside. There is nothing wrong with cutting loose on the weekends, but these tend to be more of a time of temptation. If you've been unable to avoid your temptations on the weekends, you'll need to find a way to make your weekend environments more encouraging for your self-discipline.

The first thing you'll want to do is avoid any places that might have you make poor decisions. While no one can't tell you how to live your life and your decisions are ultimately yours, and yours alone, you'll only make it more difficult on yourself if you continue to tempt yourself with old behaviors. Remember, no one is saying you can't have fun. You can still have fun, just not uninhibited fun. Keep yourself in check if you feel temptation creeping and your willpower draining.

- **On Vacation** is another time that temptation can brew. Vacations are meant to be a time to recharge yourself, but they often become stressful, from traveling to coordinating, it can feel like a job (especially if kids are involved). Some people deal with vacation stress by giving into their temptations and following their impulse to shop, drink, or gamble. These are temporary solutions to quell those burning impulses, but only self-discipline can slay these urges. Normally, I would try challenging yourself to say "no" to any tempting offers that come your way, but if you're on vacation you're expected to have fun and relax, which you still can do, just be mindful of what temptations are around and be aware of any triggers that could throw you off-track. Make your vacation environment more encouraging for developing your self-discipline by doing things you normally wouldn't do, explore the place your visiting, lay low and stay calm. This is a vacation after all. Some serenity might help restore your willpower.

Surround Yourself With People Who You Want To Be

You'd have heard the statement from Jim Rohn: "You are the average of five people you spend most time with". In fact, we may not absolutely control our decisions or discipline as much as we might like to think. Most people spend their lives believing they are fully capable of making decisions for themselves. But this is not true. Many of our decisions, we believe, are based on what we think of as common sense, while others derive from our unique experiences and perspective while spending with the people around us.

There have been studies that show that if people are surrounded by obese people, there would be significant chances that they will become obese. Your behavior will mostly get influenced by the people around you. Don't try to fool yourself that you can exercise willpower despite being surrounded by undisciplined people. Rather your whole willpower will get exhausted in resisting yourself from indulging in the self-defeating behavior; as everybody around you is carelessly involved in unhealthy behavior.

Seek out a Role Model

You can choose to get positive influence from your environment by mentally choosing out a role model. Role model would be such person, who would be already doing all the activities or has attained a level of success that you want for yourself. You need to look around and find such person, who doesn't get swayed by temptations, controls his impulses, and keeps himself focused on his goals.

When you look up to someone as your role model, it guides you in choosing your behavior moment to moment. If you choose to lose weight, and you have already sought out your role model who is slim, trim and eats healthy foods, how would you react when you are offered a pan sized pizza? You would think, "What would my role model do in such a situation? How would he handle this situation? How would he control his emotions?" These self-posed questions will immediately guide your behavior and you will refrain yourself from indulging in unhealthy behavior.

You don't need to choose a big celebrity or hire some high-profile coach while choosing your role model. He could be your close friend, neighbor, office colleague, or even your spouse or partner, provided he or she is a person, who has developed all the positive traits, that you are looking forward to adopting in your life. The best role model will act as a mirror—they will allow you to gain more self-awareness about how you are by contrasting how they act in certain situations. Whatever behaviors or actions made your role model successful will work for you. You admire their discipline, self-confidence, positive outlook towards adverse situations. Their qualities and habits can be learned, and they will make you a stronger, more disciplined person.

Design your systems by arranging things in a way that helps to build self-confidence or by choosing to meet or avoid people in a manner that helps you build your system, and you will start seeing the results sooner.

Chapter 6: Important Daily Habits To Develop Self-Discipline

The key to successfully developing your self-discipline is repetition. This is reiterated because of its importance. To do this, you will develop several daily habits. These habits will eventually become second-nature to you and you will begin doing them without even realizing it, and until your daily routine becomes habitual — again, to the point that you don't need to use any mental capacity to do it — that is when you know you're already on your way to mastering self-discipline. It may be daunting, but it isn't impossible. Follow these easy steps to get your daily routine in order. Remember, the sooner you can develop these habits, the sooner you can master self-discipline.

1. Make a Daily Schedule

Though it is pervasive, time is not an easy resource to come by. Scheduling can help us make some sense of our time and helps keep us aligned with others in our work and leisure time. Daily schedules let us block out chunks of our day, so we can stay organized in this chaotic world. With increasingly busy schedules, daily schedules can be life-savers. By creating a daily schedule, you're able to compartmentalize your time so you never miss a meeting, recital, or other event. (There are even fancy apps to do this!)

Greg always seemed busy with task after task. He wasn't an organized fellow, and his disorganized workspace and self left his co-workers feeling like he would explode if another task was handed to him. Finally, Greg realized he needed help. Amber was his casual work-buddy who shared insight. *Make yourself a schedule!* Greg decided to take her advice. He'd never thought of that himself because he was too flustered by the tasks he had to complete, which in turn caused him to miss deadlines and make other mistakes. Once he made the daily schedule, he marked off columns as "to-do" and "complete". He then organized all his tasks accordingly, leaving room for any potential changes. After a few weeks of successfully using his daily schedule, Greg discovered that he then automatically assigned his tasks to the schedule, and his productivity increased, and he was less stressed overall at work. (His co-workers appreciated it, too.)

2. Create a Daily Task (To-do) List

Much like Greg, for an effective daily schedule, you'll need to create a daily task list that requires you to actively list the tasks that you want to accomplish for that day, week, etc., and you must stick to completing these tasks. You'll want to prioritize this list so you can accomplish the most that you can within the amount of time you have for that day. These tasks should be manageable, so you can easily tick them off your list. You'll be left with the feeling of accomplishment, which will help accumulate positive motivation and fuel your self-discipline skills.

Imagine if you had to navigate your life without assistance of any kind? Where would you start? First, you have to formulate a plan, then create the list of tasks needed to accomplish your goals. Your list will help you track your progress and manage your time more efficiently, resulting in less energy spent on less important tasks so you can focus that energy on the bigger tasks at hand. By prioritizing your tasks by importance, and subsequently dividing them up in terms of how they will work towards accomplishing your larger goal, you will improve your self-discipline skills. Don't be shy about it, either. You know what needs to be done, and some of those tasks may be uncomfortable, but if they must be done in service of your larger goal, then put it on the list and get it done. You'll be thankful to have your list when it comes to reaching other goals later on.

3. Find Motivating Triggers

What motivates you to do something? There are many things that motivate us into action, including adventure, money, new experiences, and more. We are triggered by the things that make us passionate, and once you can find your motivating trigger(s), you will be able to use your impulsivity, now triggered, to be more effective at executing your self-discipline.

If you are motivated to lose weight, find a trigger that will make you choose some carrots and cardio over gorging on a three-layer cake. This is often difficult, because many people experience guilt and shame around their motivating triggers, but it's important to name these before we can ever hope to gain self-discipline. This process might take some soul-searching, but it will be well-worth the time and effort you put into it.

Triggers are a part of everyday life. Some people have more triggers than others; some people are triggered more easily or frequently. Triggers can be difficult to understand, but self-discipline can help curb those triggers that otherwise would send someone into a frenzy of ineffective or unwanted behavior. There is underlying trauma that causes the triggers, and the reaction in turn is to indulge oneself in whatever manner we see fit. This could be drinking, overeating, using drugs, or other behaviors that are the reactions to the triggers that person is experiencing.

Take the story of Jerry, who had a traumatic experience as a child that caused him to dabble in drugs for most of his teen years and all of his adult life. Now twenty-nine years old, Jerry would use drugs whenever he was triggered, which was usually at home, where he lived with his aunt, who was also a user. His home environment was triggering, and the cycle needed to be broken. One of Jerry's friends, Reed, offered him a place to stay so he wouldn't be triggered by his aunt and the drug use at home. Once Jerry eliminated his trigger, he was able to focus on his willpower to not use drugs more effectively because his trigger no longer prodded him.

4. Practice Self-denial

While some may see this tip as masochistic, practicing self-denial is quite valid and useful when it comes to developing effective daily self-disciplinary habits. Self-denial is exactly what it sounds like—you choose something that you impulsively want and deny yourself it. The neurological reward center will rewire itself if conditioned and left to be denied a reward. Your brain will also adjust to the reward denial system, and eventually your impulse to do said thing is gone.

If self-denial is too harsh a term for you, try thinking of it as self-restraint from your desire for instant gratification. This is one of the tougher skills to practice, particularly if you have a lot of impulsivities. The key to successfully implementing self-denial into your routine is to think of something that you desire in the moment or want to get on a regular basis and then deny yourself that very thing for, say, one month. It could be anything from that morning latte or an extra slice of cake to staying up late binging over late night TV shows. Once you can successfully abstain from your indulgences for that one month, continue practicing until you are ready to reward yourself, which can be whatever you feel it should be. You know how much work you put into it. Remember, you can't lie to yourself, because in the end you only cheat yourself. Do your best to avoid your triggers and try using self-denial and once you feel comfortable with it, you'll see that you'll be well on your way to mastering self-discipline.

5. Do Something Active

It's proven that physical activity is one of the best ways to maintain not only your physical health but also your mental health. Medical science has shown that just a few minutes of aerobic exercise flood endorphins to your neurological receptors, feeding your brain with "happy" feelings. Exercise is recommended as part of your self-discipline training because it is a routine that you can easily integrate into your life.

This is the story of Danika, who had always felt depressed. She disliked going outdoors and spent most of her time in her room in front of the television or her computer monitor. She never exercised, despite her doctor's advice. She was thirty-three when a routine doctor appointment gave her quite a scare—she was at high-risk for diabetes. She needed to change her diet and exercise. Following doctor's instructions, Danika devised a diet, which she was not fond of at first, and she came up with an exercise routine. Thirty minutes a day was all she needed to do. She included some cardio exercise and began walking around her neighborhood in the evenings. After a few months of sticking to her regimen, Danika not only reduced her risk for diabetes, but she also lost weight and reported that she wasn't feeling so depressed. As Danika discovered, you'll be surprised by what a bit of activity will do for your body and mind.

EXERCISE: Develop an exercise routine and commit to following it as it's scheduled. No one is expecting you to hit the gym seven days a week though- even alternate days of exercise can help you. Moreover, ten to thirty minutes a day is all you need. This is enough time to do some stretches, cardio exercises, and maybe even some meditation. If you're into something a little more rigorous, you could ride a bike or go run/jog/walk briskly as part of your morning or evening routine. Following an exercise regimen will help you develop your self-discipline in no time.

6. Don't wait till you "feel right".

Improving your self-discipline means changing up your normal routine, which can be uncomfortable and awkward. Charles Duhigg, author of *The Power of Habit*, explains that your behaviors are traced to a part of the brain called the basal ganglia - a portion of the brain associated with emotions, patterns, and memories. On the other hand, decisions are made in the prefrontal cortex, a completely different area responsible for all executive functions of brain. When a behavior becomes a habit, we stop using our decision-making skills and instead function on auto-pilot. Therefore, breaking a bad habit and building a new habit not only requires us to make active decisions, it will feel wrong. Your brain will resist the change in favor of what it has been programmed to do. So, what is the solution? Embrace the wrong, as it is simply not feeling right. Acknowledge that it will take a while for your new regime to feel right or good or natural. Keep practicing and it will happen soon.

7. Practice Mindfulness.

Don't just think this as some mystical stuff, because mindfulness is now proven by neuroscience as a panacea for the overall wellbeing of humans. Brain imaging studies show that an eight-week course in mindfulness-based stress reduction can be enough to shrink the part of the brain known as the amygdala. That is a primal region of the brain associated with fear and emotion and involved in the body's stress response. Also, the prefrontal cortex—associated with executive functions such as awareness, concentration, and decision-making—becomes thicker. Similar to the way physical exercise creates changes in your muscles, mindfulness training creates changes in your brain. These changes in your brain structure produce huge number of benefits, including reduction in stress and anxiety, better sleep, happier relationships, and better focus and concentration, just to list a few.

Kelly McGonigal, researcher and author of *Willpower Instinct* specifies a huge number of benefits of mindfulness and the results don't take long to appear. She explains the benefits of mindfulness for developing self-discipline in below words:

> It doesn't take a lifetime of meditation to change the brain. One study found that just three hours of meditation practice led to improved attention and self-control. After

eleven hours, researchers could see those changes in the brain. The new meditators had increased neural connections between regions of the brain important for staying focused, ignoring distractions, and controlling impulses. Another study found that eight weeks of daily meditation practice led to increased self-awareness in everyday life, as well as increased gray matter in corresponding areas of the brain.

It may seem incredible that our brains can reshape themselves so quickly, but meditation increases blood flow to the prefrontal cortex, in much the same way that lifting weights increases blood flow to your muscles. The brain appears to adapt to exercise in the same way that muscles do, getting both bigger and faster to get better at what you ask of it. So if you're ready to train your brain, the following meditation technique will get the blood rushing to your prefrontal cortex—the closest we can get to speeding up evolution, and making the most of our brains' potential.

8. First Feeling of Fatigue Is An Illusion

How do you react when you feel tired while doing your workout? Most people think that they are tired and then stop. But the reality is that you are not really physically tired, at the first feeling of fatigue. Studies show that the first feeling of fatigue is merely an emotion, not the signal that your body is exhausted and can't go on any longer.

Developing self-discipline and mental toughness isn't just about being resilient. It's also about learning to access your reserve tank when you think you just can't go any further. We all think we know our limits. Whether you're exercising, studying, or just trying to break a bad habit, there's always that moment when you feel like you are done and there is no more left in you. But there is a concept in Navy SEAL, which they say as 40% Rule. They say, when your mind is telling you you're done, you're really only 40% done. It means you are still left with more than half of your energy in your body.

You can learn how to exert more self-discipline when you decide to go past the first feeling of fatigue and see how much further you can push yourself. If you want to stretch out your workout for a longer period, don't be afraid to go past your original limits and see if you can push a little bit more.

In fact, you are more capable than you realize, but you have to fight off the mental blocks you've established over the years. You can run farther, you can learn more, and you can resist your vices longer. The next time you feel like giving up, remember, you've still got 60% left.

The words of Joe De Sena, the originator of one of the toughest race named Spartan Race and author of the book *Spartan Up* will definitely raise your morale to do something challenging. He mentions: *"Challenging yourself to accomplish more than you know you can is never stupid — it helps show you what you are capable of. It creates a new frame of reference, one you* can draw upon in the face of other things that are perceived as being tough in your life. It shows you possibilities you didn't know existed."

Chapter 7: Building Systems to Stay On Track

If you're going to be successful at mastering self-discipline, you'll need to build systems that will help you stay on track. From simple notes to sophisticated digital apps that will help you maintain your daily routines. Once you have a system for yourself in place, it will make it much easier to stay on-track, no matter what methods you use. Let's take a look at some of the most successful tools you can use to build your self-discipline training system.

- **Calendars & Planners** are tried and trusted by many trying to keep their lives organized, calendars and planners are one of the strongest tools in your toolbox. Use these to remind yourself of your routines, so that your training is always at the forefront of your mind throughout the day/week/month. You can use either traditional or digital calendars and planners, of which there are a variety to choose from.

- **Alarms** are invaluable when it comes to reminders, which will help keep you on track when you have to do something important. Set an alarm to wake up and start your morning routine. Set an alarm to denote each portion of your routine. One for your midday meeting. For your afternoon break. For your kid's recital. For your evening routine and, of course, for bedtime. Often, we simply need a quick nudge to start something and alarms just do that. Alarms immediately make us aware of the action to be taken at a particular time. And since it comes from somewhere outside of us, that prompts many people psychologically to take action, as if there is some outside pressure.

Alarms will become your best friend and will elevate your self-discipline, as it forces you to conform your life to the constraints of time, and when you're forced to think about what you have to do and how much time you have to do it in, you build awareness, which is a huge step towards mastering self-discipline.

- **Self-discipline Apps** are used in the twenty-first century, since things are mostly done digitally now, so it's no surprise that there is a wide array of mobile apps available that will help you with everything from work and efficiency to managing your mind and body. These are, of course, used in conjunction with you doing the actual work. (Don't expect the app to do it for you.) Some of the more popular apps include Bloom, Luminosity, SimpleMind+, Weekdone, 30/30, Headspace, and 7-Minute Workout among others.

- **Your Social Network** doesn't mean only your Facebook, Twitter, or other online pals. This means all your friends, family, and colleagues in real-life that you can rely on to help you with your routine, whether it's reminding you to eat healthier or joining you for an exercise session. (Just to clarify: not saying that you can't have a strong network of people online that you can turn to for support, but for the sake of this section, this is in reference to your real-life connections.) Nobody ever said that solitude was an ingredient for self-discipline. Self-discipline can sometimes be infectious, and your routines may become more exciting if you get to experience it with a friend or loved one. The people close to you will also be able to keep you on track and call you out if needed.

However, if you find difficulty in finding a real-life connection to help you awaken your inner self-control, or maybe you are initially hesitant to approach someone – no worries, technology is there to help you. Few apps do a wonderful job to build social accountability. I remember one app called Strava, which is a social network for athletes. If you are interested in physical fitness, but lack discipline, this app can help you. Though it can be used for a number of sporting activities, but most popular tracked activities are running and cycling. You just record your activity on Strava feed, and your friends and followers can share their own races and workouts, applause for great performances and leave comments on each other's activities.

Whatever system(s) you choose for your routines, you have to be comfortable doing the routines, otherwise you risk giving up. While it's good to have ambitious goals for your self-discipline, remember to start small and work up to the bigger, more difficult goals. For example, you may want to lose fifty pounds. That's no easy feat, but you'll need to develop your routines for accomplishing this. Now, you're not going to lose fifty pounds in two weeks or even two months (if you do it safely), and it's going to take willpower over the period of time you're dieting to eat right and exercise as per your routine. This building of self-discipline will result in you successfully shedding the weight you wanted to. It may have been daunting at first, but by breaking it down over time, it becomes smaller, more feasible goals that you can track and see your progress, which will confirm all your hard work as you move forward.

Let's take a look at the story of Rose, who wanted to lose weight but lacked self-control when it came to eating. She couldn't help herself, but she would indulge her taste buds' every whim. She ate that way her whole life, and now she was facing diabetes and heart disease, so her doctor told her she had to go on a diet, get exercise, and refrain from those eating impulses. Now granted the eating impulse was due to her anxiety, so she learned some relaxation techniques she could use to quell the anxiety enough to not turn to food. Herein lies the key: Rose used her willpower to do the relaxation exercise over eating. She had to practice, she even faltered a few times, but she eventually was able to overcome her anxiety-eating.

It is possible to make yourself go against what it naturally is inclined to do. Police officers face hails of bullets in the streets, yet they make themselves go into the fray. Military personnel also force themselves into situations when fear or anxiety or even good judgement tell them to go the other way. For good or ill, self-discipline works in many ways for people. It is defined by their individual goals, which only they can make or break.

Self-discipline is the tool that has the power to develop one of the toughest types of people on the planet– the Navy SEALs. The next chapter of the book will help you understand how they build their mental toughness.

Chapter 8: Four Pillars of Mental Toughness of a Navy SEAL

Have you ever pursued something so relentlessly that no matter what obstacles stood in your way you just kept pushing forward? That's what mental toughness is about. It's about responding resiliently to overwhelming odds that are stacked against you.

A person who is mentally tough feels deep within their core that they can stretch themselves way far than they think of. They push through adversity and difficulties with determination, urgency, and focused effort — without ever losing hope, confidence or self-belief.

Whether you are starting out on your journey to self-discipline or you have taken a few steps already on this path, it is worth knowing how the world's toughest people become that way. You will learn about the secret of mental toughness of the Navy SEALs.

United States Navy SEALs are considered one of the most trained soldiers on the planet and their training is considered one of the toughest military trainings in the world. What neurologists found is that it's not always those who are physically strong, but more importantly those who are also mentally strong as well, when it comes to overall strength of a human being. The neuroscience division of the Navy SEAL developed a handbook for the SEALs called *The Four Pillars of Mental Toughness*, which laid out the four tenets that one needs to gain control over, calling for strong self-discipline in order to do so. You can imagine the level of mental toughness of Navy SEAL, from the words of Marcus Luttrell former United States Navy Seal, when he describes: *"To break a Navy Seal, you have to kill us. That's why we can make it into our training. That's why we can call ourselves Seals because the only way you're gonna break us is to kill us."*

Not only do these principles apply to Navy SEALs, but they have also been proven to work for musicians, professional athletes, and successful entrepreneurs.

Below are the four pillars of mental toughness of Navy SEALs.

1. **Setting Goals**: Navy SEAL candidates are trained to focus primarily on the short-term goals – meaning whatever is handed over to them, they just need to finish that activity without worrying about the other future part of that activity. Instead of focusing on the larger picture of everything that had to be done that day or that week, they focused on one task at a time. That allows them to stay relaxed and engaged in that activity only and not to worry or stress about what needs to be done next. This practice helps to turn off the part of brain that causes you stress and thus allows you to finish the work at hand. This practice can be made easily applicable to anything field, be it sports, studies or your high-profile business goals – anything. If you simply focus on the workout you are doing today, without worry about the whole next week, you will not get frustrated by the daunting task.

2. **Mental Visualization**: Mentally visualizing the process of doing the things in your mind before the real work is widely used in sports already and studies have shown that mental rehearsal improves the performance. Navy SEALs have this second tenet of mental visualization in their arsenal. By visualizing a

scenario, you are essentially practicing it. It is just as important as doing the real thing. Regular periods of visualization can help provide you with greater clarity about your goals and about the actions you need to take to achieve them. This clarity of mind is likely to provide you with more certainty and self-assurance moving forward.

For artists, performance anxiety is an issue. To overcome this fear, the artist say musician just mentally envision their full performance and would repeat this over and over again. They would imagine plucking the notes and performing live in front of audience and seeing the whole audience giving them a standing ovation at the end of performance. By mentally seeing the performance repeatedly you mind starts to feel it like reality and when the time comes for the real performance, this practice is already engraved in your brain so well, that you just play it another time without any anxiety. Navy SEAL mentally visualize the real-life challenge that may come in the war kind of situation and envision how they would conquer over the enemy in such situations.

3. **Positive Self-Talk**: Some studies show that people talk to themselves on average of 800-1600 words per minute. Depending on your mood, your self-talk can also affect your performance for the day. By staying positive, you will be able to make it through any hardship. Navy SEALs know very well that they may be required to face any tough situation or challenge while on their duty. No matter difficult the situation is, they learn to tell themselves, 'Yes, you can do it'. Words have immense power as they drive your thoughts. With positive self-talk, you generate empowering thoughts, and these thoughts drive your behavior and action in any situation. Navy SEALs are trained to sail through the toughest situations, even when their life is at stake, thanks to the positive self-talk they keep telling themselves.

4. **Arousal Control**: Controlling your mental state is easier said than done. However, the successful Seals that make it through training attribute a lot of this to breathing exercises they call the 4×4 technique, where they inhale for 4 seconds and exhale for 4 seconds as well. By doing this, you essentially lower your heart rate at its resting state. It is a great technique at calming you down when your senses are

heightened. For performance artists, this technique can be applied before a performance. By using this arousal control technique, you can diminish the natural adrenaline jitters of performing, allowing you to stay calm and perform with less tension and anxiety. Navy SEALs need to have absolute control over their impulsive behavior, because lack of this may jeopardize the mission of the whole group and even put the lives of other colleagues in danger.

By following the above four tenets, the Navy SEALs develop the kind of mental toughness that is needed to handle the toughest war like conditions in even most adverse climatic conditions. Even if someone doesn't want to pursue Navy SEAL as a career, he or she can apply these principles of mental toughness in any domain.

Chapter 9: Practical Strategies to Master Self-Discipline

Now let's talk about few practical strategies that you can incorporate in your daily life. Everyone has busy lives, and change takes time and is not easy. In this section, we'll review some practical ways you can master self-discipline in your everyday life.

EXERCISE: Follow these simple strategies when mastering self-discipline.

1. Schedule one task for the same time every day. This can be at home or work. It should not take more than 15 minutes to complete. Continue to do this for eight weeks to build a routine. Now repeat this for other tasks.

2. Time management is an important tool in mastering self-discipline and learning how to wisely use your time also helps you use your energy more efficiently. When working, think

"smarter, not harder", which means that when you assign yourself a task to complete, don't spend large chunks of time working. Work diligently for shorter periods and take breaks to relieve yourself and let your brain have a moment to recoup.

There is a technique called the Pomodoro technique that is popularly used for enhancing productivity. Under the Pomodoro technique, you work for a stretch of 25 minutes, then you take a break for 5 minutes. After total three rounds of this 25 minutes work and five minutes break, you then go for a longer break of fifteen minutes. In each break time, you just get disengaged from your work, maybe have a brief walk around your workstation. This helps your brain to relax and engage in the work afresh after the break. There is an app that helps you to schedule this work and break schedule known as Clockwork Tomato[6], that you can use to apply this technique.

3. Keeping a log of your progress is incredibly useful. Not only does a log show you a definitive record of what you've accomplished, but it tracks your journey so you can see what is working and what needs to be adjusted. This is also a good place to put your thoughts throughout this process.

4. If you're feeling discouraged, check in with yourself to make sure that you're feeling aligned with your goals. Use positive self-talk to build yourself up so you can tackle the task at hand.

5. One of the oldest, albeit most difficult, tricks to mastering self-discipline is associating a new habit with an old one. Let's say your goal is to quit smoking cigarettes. It's a terrible habit to try to break, but one way some people overcome their cravings is by associating a new

habit – say, eating carrot sticks – with the old habit of smoking, effectively replacing the old (bad) habit with the new (good) habit.

6. Find a strong role model that has it together. See if they're willing to impart any wisdom in the ways of self-discipline. People like to have their brains picked, and any help you can get on your journey is welcome.

7. Read Literature on building self-discipline. Controlling your urges is not an easy task, and often you will get demoralized to take further action. Here you would need some dose of instant motivation and books helps you to stay on track. Sometimes even a single piece of advice in any good book can help you to energize and take consistent action towards your goals. You would have heard the quote from legend Zig Ziglar saying: *"People often say that motivation doesn't last. Well, neither does bathing - that's why we recommend it daily."*

8. Schedule breaks, treats, and rewards for yourself. Self-discipline does not mean your new regimen needs to be entirely cold turkey, hard core, or drill sergeant-like in execution. In fact, pushing yourself too harsh often results in failures, disappointments, and giving into your old ways. While practicing self-control, schedule specific breaks, treats, and rewards for yourself. If you are dieting, fix Sunday as your cheat day, when you can eat whatever you want. Self-discipline is a hard and long-term game. Don't forget to reward your efforts on the journey.

9. Watch YouTube videos on personal development. Watching videos is one of the best methods for deeper understanding, because here you use your multiple senses in learning. You look through your eyes, hear through your ears, and it leaves a long-term impression on your brain. Moreover, since you have to sit to watch, you can't do multitasking with it, so it

helps to let the message drilled deeply into your nerves. Just spend 40 seconds watching this inspiring video from Will Smith. Just look at the expression and voice tonality, and you will understand how strongly Smith has built his self-control muscles.

https://www.youtube.com/watch?v=doqS3 5FfcUE

10. Forgive yourself and move forward. Instituting a new way of thinking won't always go according to plan. You will have ups and downs, sometimes great successes, and then often failures too. The key is to keep moving forward. When you have a setback, acknowledge what caused it and move on. It is easy to get wrapped up in guilt, anger, or frustration, but these emotions will not help build improve self-discipline. Instead, use the hiccups in your plan as learning experiences for the future. Forgive yourself and get back in the game as

soon as you can. The longer you're off your game, the harder it is to keep going in a positive direction.

Incorporate Self-Discipline in Different Areas of Your Life

Self-discipline is not a singular entity that only applies to one area of your life. When you use self-discipline at home with your family looks different than it does at work with your colleagues, but you're still applying the techniques regardless of the setting. By utilizing the skills you learned in here, you will be able to set goals in all areas of your life, whether you're trying for a promotion at work or you're trying to be a better person for yourself and your family.

Some of the areas where you can practice self-discipline include:

- Getting some form of activity/exercise everyday
- Eating more healthily or dieting
- Managing interpersonal relationships (e.g.; spouse, children, friends, bosses, etc.)
- Setting goals and a routine

- Accomplishing tasks
- Negotiating deals
- Helping others
- Having patience with people, electronics, and things you can't control
- Dealing with difficult situations (remember the SEALs!)

There are countless ways that self-discipline can be applied to many, if not all, areas of your life. It's up to you to decide how you want to develop your self-discipline and where you want to apply it, the above ways are merely a jumping-off point for you. This is one of the greatest aspects of learning self-discipline, you can use any or all of the tips in this book for whatever your goals are. This is about you. You want to accomplish something, this book is merely here to help guide you, but in the end, you're doing the work, you're reaping the benefits. The question is, what are you going to do about it? Whether you're a Navy SEAL or a regular Joe (or Jane), some area of your life could benefit from self-discipline.

EXERCISE: Make a list of some of the areas of your life where self-discipline could improve your life. Then list ways you could practice self-discipline in those areas. Think about the various self-discipline techniques that can be incorporated into each area of your life.

Self-Discipline for Personal & Spiritual Growth

If there's anything you gain from mastering self-discipline, it's gaining personal and spiritual growth. Self-discipline is not only a way for us to measure ourselves and how much of what the world throws at us we can take, it is also a way for us to learn more about ourselves so that we can become better than we were. This is not only a personal journey, but one that, regardless of your beliefs, is a spiritual one.

Self-discipline lends itself to the highest echelons of the human spirit, giving those with it the ability to accomplish great things and inspire others to do the same. Many people shy away from the journey because of how daunting it is to change one's lifestyle in pursuit of happiness. Without self-discipline, we would be running amok with no semblance of order. All the worthiest ideas throughout history would never have made it into the folds of time if not for those with the self-discipline to inquire, discover, and create.

Really think about who you are, what you want out of life, and how you want to get there. You already possess self-discipline, it just needs a little bit of coaxing to come out. And that's what this book will hopefully do for you. There are so many things about self-discipline that cannot be simply broken down into a few sentences here, because part of learning self-discipline is actually doing it (and practicing it every day). Don't forget that to be successful with self-discipline you must willingly enter into the experience so that you can practice these skills.

While self-discipline needs to be developed, it is an innate feature in humans, which we cannot deny ourselves. It is a part of what makes us whole, what makes us human. If we cannot achieve that, we are incomplete. It is imperative that you use the tools, tips, and techniques presented in this book to master self-discipline for yourself, so you can lead a happier, more productive personal and professional life. Because, as Jim Rohn rightly said once:

"Discipline is the bridge between goals and accomplishments"

In Conclusion

The subject of self-discipline has fascinated humans since the great philosophers of ancient civilizations first pondered what it meant for one to "be". Self-discipline helps us understand ourselves and our place in the world. Without self-discipline, failure for humanity would be imminent.

It is with great hope that this book will help many people master self-discipline and begin to lead happier lives as a result of the skills in here. This book is not comprehensive and there is a wide variety of other tips, tools, and topics on self-discipline, many of which are much more in-depth than this writing. However, the objective of this book is to get you started with the utmost essential tools that you would need to embark upon your journey towards self-discipline.

I wish you a great luck.

Copyright © 2018 by Pollux Andrews

All rights reserved. No part of this book may be reproduced in any form without permission in writing from the author.

No part of this publication may be reproduced or transmitted in any form or by any means, mechanical or electronic, including photocopying or recording, or by any information storage and retrieval system, or transmitted by email or by any other means whatsoever without permission in writing from the author.

DISCLAIMER

While all attempts have been made to verify the information provided in this publication, the author does not assume any responsibility for errors, omissions, or contrary interpretations of the subject matter herein.

The views expressed are those of the author alone and should not be taken as expert instruction or commands. The reader is responsible for his or her own actions.

The author makes no representations or warranties with respect to the accuracy or completeness of the contents of this work and specifically disclaims all warranties, including without limitation warranties of fitness for a particular purpose. No warranty may be created or extended by sales or promotional materials. The advice and recipes contained herein may not be suitable for everyone. This work is sold with the understanding that the author is not engaged in rendering medical, legal or other professional advice or services. If professional assistance is required, the services of a competent professional person should be sought. The author shall not be liable for damages arising here from. The fact that an individual, organization of website is referred to in this work as a citation and/or potential source of further information does not mean that the author endorses the information the individual, organization to website may provide or recommendations they/it may make. Further, readers should be aware that Internet websites listed in this work might have changed or disappeared between when this work was written and when it is read.

Adherence to all applicable laws and regulations, including international, federal, state, and local governing professional licensing, business practices, advertising, and all other aspects of doing business in any jurisdiction in the world is the sole responsibility of the purchaser or reader.

86016681R00063

Made in the USA
San Bernardino, CA
24 August 2018